General
Maxims
of
Teaching

A. BRONSON ALCOTT
(1799–1888)

General Maxims

of

Teaching

*By Which to Regulate the
Instructor's Practice in Instruction*

—❧—

BY A. BRONSON ALCOTT

APPLEWOOD BOOKS

CARLISLE, MASSACHUSETTS

From the original journal of A. Bronson Alcott, 1826.

Image of Temple School and frontispiece portrait
image of A. Bronson Alcott used by permission
of Louisa May Alcott's Orchard House.

Thank you for purchasing an Applewood book.
Applewood reprints America's lively classics—
books from the past that are still of
interest to modern readers.
For a free copy of our current catalog,
please write to: Applewood Books,
Box 27, Carlisle, MA 01741,
or visit us at www.awb.com.

ISBN: 978-1-4290-9543-3

10 9 8 7 6 5 4 3 2 1

MANUFACTURED IN THE UNITED STATES OF AMERICA
WITH AMERICAN-MADE MATERIALS

GENERAL MAXIMS OF TEACHING

Amos Bronson Alcott (1799–1888) was an American educator and transcendentalist philosopher. He combined his love of both pursuits when he developed his "58 Maxims of Teaching" in 1826. These aphorisms guided Alcott's own educational techniques throughout his professional life. Over the course of his career, he established a number of successful schools, including one of America's first adult continuing-education facilities, the Concord School of Philosophy and Literature, in Massachusetts. Alcott's most famous children's school, the Temple School, in Boston, incorporated these maxims within its curriculum from 1834 until 1839.

The Temple School was revolutionary in its educational approach; it was the first American school to offer physical-education classes, field trips, and recess as aspects of education. Traditional teaching methods in the nineteenth century did not allow students to ask questions; instead, the emphasis was on rote learning, with order enforced using corporal punishment. In contrast, Alcott's "Maxims" all promote an objective, whole-person approach to education that helps build reason and kindness in the classroom—a method that continues to inspire educators today. Though in his own time Alcott was often seen as radical for supporting such ideas, we continue to see his legacy preserved and embraced in both private schools and the public-school systems of today.

1.

To teach, with a sense of
accountableness to the profession

2.

To teach, with reference
to eternity

3.

To teach, as an agent of
the Great Instructor

4.

To teach, depending on the
Divine Blessings for success

5.

To teach, as the former of
Character and the promoter of
the collective happiness of Man

6.

To teach, to subserve the
great cause of philanthropy
and benevolence

7.

To teach, distinct from
all sinister, sectarian and
oppressive principles

8.

To teach, with charitable
feelings toward all rational
and animal beings

9.

To teach, distinct from prejudice,
from veneration of antiquity,
and from excess of novelty

10.

To teach, to improve the
science of instruction and mind

11.

To teach, duly appreciating
the importance of the profession

12.

To teach, awed by the clamours
of ignorance, yet governed
by the dictates of wisdom

13.

To teach, nothing from
subservience to custom

14.

To teach, with unremitted
solicitude and faithfulness

15.

To teach, appreciating the
value of the beings to whom
instruction is given

16.

To teach, regarding
the matter as well as the
manner of instruction

17.

To teach, that alone
which is useful

18.

To teach, in imitation
of the Saviour

19.

To teach, by exact
uniform example

20.

To teach, in the
inductive method

21.

To teach, gradually and
understandingly, by the shortest
steps, from the more easy
and known, to the more
difficult and unknown

22.

To teach, by the exercise
of reason

23.

To teach, illustrating by sensible
and tangible objects

24.

To teach, by clear and
copious explanation

25.

To teach, by strict
adherence to system

26.

To teach, by simple and plain
unambiguous language

27.

To teach, by short and
perfectly obtained lessons

28.

To teach, by encouragement

29.

To teach, but one thing
at the same time

30.

To teach, interestingly

31.

To teach, principally a knowledge
of things, not of words–of ideas,
not names

32.

To teach, by consulting in
the arrangement of lessons, that
proportion of variety which is
adapted to the genius and habits
of the young mind

33.

To teach, by keeping
curiosity awake

34.

To teach, nothing that pupils
can teach themselves

35.

To teach, as much as
possible by analysis

36.

To teach, by exciting a laudable
ambition for excellence, guarding
against its opposite

37.

To teach, endeavouring to make pupils feel their importance by the hope which mankind placed in their conduct

38.

To teach, endeavouring to preserve the understanding from implicit belief, and to secure the habit of independence of thought and of feeling

39.

To teach, endeavouring to invigorate and bring into exercise all the intellectual, moral, and physical powers

40.

To teach, attempting to
associate with literature the
idea and perception of pleasure

41.

To teach, attempting to
induce the laudable ambition
of progressive improvement

42.

To teach, by consulting
the feelings of scholars

43.

To teach, with animation
and interest

44.

To teach, by furnishing
constant, useful, and as much as
possible, pleasing employment

45.

To teach, treating pupils
with uniform familiarity,
and patience, and with
the greatest kindness,
tenderness, and respect

46.

To teach, by cultivating the
moral, and sympathetic
feelings and affections

47.

To teach, by cultivating the
collective happiness of the school.

48.

To teach, by persuasion,
not by coercion

49.

To teach, by comparison and contrast

50.

To teach, by allusion to familiar
objects and occurrences

51.

To teach, without indolence
and discouragement

52.

To teach, pupils to teach themselves

53.

To teach, by intermingling
questions with instruction

54.

To teach, with relation to the
practical business of life

55.

To teach, endeavouring
to fix things in the understanding
rather than words in the memory

56.

To teach, without bringing pupils in comparison with one another, or touching the spring of personal emulation

57.

To teach, with reference to habit

58.

To teach, with Independence